Date Due			
DEC 7			
OCT 3	4		

1844

Adler, Irving and Ruth

The calendar

The "Reason Why" Books

THE CALENDAR

Irving and Ruth Adler

The John Day Company   New York

The "Reason Why" Books
by Irving and Ruth Adler

Copyright © 1967 by Irving and Ruth Adler

1844   TITLE II

Library of Congress Catalogue Card Number: 67-23865

PRINTED IN THE UNITED STATES OF AMERICA

Third Impression

Contents

S	M	T	W
1	2	3	4

Everyone Uses a Calendar

One year your birthday may fall on a Monday. Another year your birthday may fall on a Saturday. You have no trouble knowing when your birthday comes each year. You know this with the help of a calendar.

Thanksgiving Day always falls on the fourth Thursday of November. The fourth Thursday might be any day from November 22 through November 28. We have no trouble knowing when Thanksgiving Day comes each year. We know this with the help of a calendar.

Farmers use a calendar to help them decide when to plant and harvest their

8	9	10	1
15	16	17	1
22	23	24	2
29	30	31	New

V	T	F	S
↓	5	6	7
1	12	13	14
8	19	20	21
5	26	27	28

crops. Highway departments use a calendar to know when to take out their snow plows and when to store them again. Airlines, steamship lines, bus lines and railroads all use a calendar to guide them in planning when airplanes, steamships, buses and trains will leave and arrive. Banks and schools use a calendar to guide them in planning their work.

This book will tell you what a calendar is. It will tell you about the earliest calendars made by people a long time ago and about how the calendar we use came to be. It will also tell you about other calendars that are used by other people today. And it will show you how to make a calendar that you can use for fifty years.

Moon   First Quarter   Full Moon   Last Quarter

th   14th   22nd   1st & 30th

Why People Needed a Calendar

Earliest man got his food by hunting and fishing and by gathering fruits, nuts, berries and roots. He observed that there were times when his food supply was scarce. His food supply was good when the weather was warm and there was lots of rain. Food was scarce when the weather was cold or there was little rain. He observed that a period of cold weather in a particular place was followed by a period of warm weather in that place. Also, a period of warm weather was, in turn, followed by a period of cold weather. By keeping track of these periods of cold and warm weather, he made a crude calendar. He used it to guide him in moving from place to place, so that he would always have enough to eat.

Periods of cold weather were followed by periods of warm weather.

When man became a farmer and settled down in one place he observed that there was a best time for planting his crops. This was when the trees and ground were covered with a new green cover after having been bare during a long period of cold. He observed that there was a best time to harvest his crops. This was before it turned cold again and his crops froze. He observed that times of cold, when the earth was bare, were followed by warm weather when plants began to grow again. He celebrated the return of greenness which was the time for planting. He celebrated harvest time and the time when cold returned once again. These celebrations were man's first religious holidays. The ancient farmer needed a calendar to guide him in the planting and harvesting of his crops and the celebration of his religious holidays.

Celebrating a religious holiday in ancient Egypt

What Is a Calendar?

Early man noticed that there were certain events that happened over and over again. Some of these were events in his daily life. Some of these were events he saw happening in the sky.

In his daily life, he noticed that periods when he slept were followed by periods when he was awake. And periods of waking were, in turn, followed by periods of sleeping. He noticed the changes of seasons from winter to spring to summer to fall and back to winter again. He noticed that certain rivers flooded their banks over and over again according to a regular pattern.

In the sky, he noticed that periods of daylight, when he was awake, were followed by periods of darkness, when he slept. He noticed the *day*. He noticed that the moon did not always look the same and that the changes

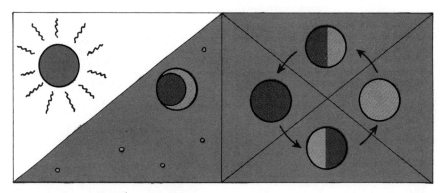

Darkness follows daylight and daylight follows darkness. This gives us the *day*.

The moon changes its appearance in a regular pattern. This gives us the *month*.

in the way the moon looked followed a regular pattern. He noticed the *month*. He noticed that, from day to day, the stars changed their positions in the sky according to a regular pattern. He noticed that, from day to day, the sun did not rise in the same place in the east nor set in the same place in the west. From day to day, the rising place of the sun moved farther and farther north until it reached a certain place. Then the rising place of the sun began to move south. It continued to move south until it reached a certain place and then began to move north again. He noticed that this movement of the sun followed a regular pattern that was like the pattern of the seasons. He noticed the *year*. He then tried to make an orderly plan for putting together days and months into a year. This orderly plan is called a calendar.

If the sky looked like this at night . . .

. . . then it looked like this at the same time of the night six months later.

The night sky changes from day to day. This gives us the *year*.

9

The Day

The people who lived long ago noticed that the stars at night, like the sun during the day, rose in the east and set in the west. This made them think that the sun and the stars were turning around the earth. We now know that this isn't so. It only looks that way.

It looks as though the sun and the stars are turning around the earth because the earth is a great spinning ball. It spins around an imaginary line that passes through its center. This line is called the earth's *axis* (AX-iss). The North Pole is at one end of the axis. The South Pole is at the other end of the axis. The *equator* (ee-KWAY-tur) is a circle around the earth, halfway between the North and South Poles.

North Pole

AXIS

EQUATOR

South Pole

The earth spins around an imaginary line that passes through its center. This line is called the earth's *axis.*

10

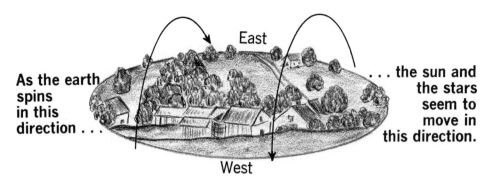

As the earth spins in this direction . . .

East

. . . the sun and the stars seem to move in this direction.

West

As the earth spins on its axis, the sun and the stars seem to move across the sky from east to west. They seem to move from east to west because the earth is spinning from west to east. So the sun and the stars seem to rise in the east, set in the west and then rise in the east again. The amount of time from one sunrise to the next sunrise is about equal to the length of time we call a day. A day is divided into twenty-four equal parts called *hours.*

The Year

At the same time that the earth spins around its axis, it also moves through space in a path around the sun. The path, which is almost a circle, is called the earth's *orbit* (OR-bit). The earth makes a complete trip in its orbit around the sun in a year. The length of time for this trip is called a sun year or *solar* (SO-lur) year. There are about 365¼ days in a solar year.

The earth's axis does not stand up straight on the path the earth follows around the sun. It is tilted. The axis is

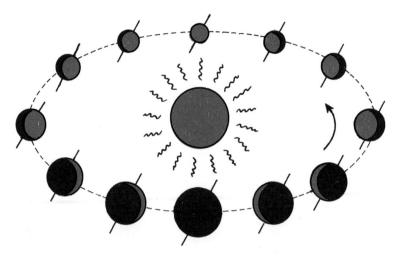

The tilt of the earth's axis as the earth moves in its orbit around the sun

always tilted in the same direction because the earth is spinning around it. The picture above shows the tilt of the earth's axis as the earth moves in its orbit around the sun.

The tilt of the earth's axis and the earth's motion around the sun cause the seasons. In the first picture on page 13, the North Pole is tilted toward the sun. When the earth is in this position, the half of the earth that is north of the equator gets a lot of sunlight and it is summer there. The sun reaches its rising place that is farthest to the north at about this time. In the north, each day has more hours of daylight than darkness at this time, too. When the earth is in this position, the South Pole is tilted away from the sun. Then the half of the earth that is south of the equator gets only a small amount of sunlight and it is winter there.

The second picture below shows the tilt of the earth's axis a half year later. Then the North Pole is tilted away from the sun and it is winter north of the equator. The South Pole is tilted toward the sun and it is summer south of the equator. The sun reaches its rising place that is farthest to the south at about this time. Places south of the equator have more hours of daylight than darkness at this time. At the same time, each day, in the north, has fewer hours of daylight than darkness.

When the earth is halfway between the positions in the two pictures, days and nights are of equal length and spring and fall begin. The times of the year when this happens are called the *equinoxes* (EE-kwuh-nox-is).

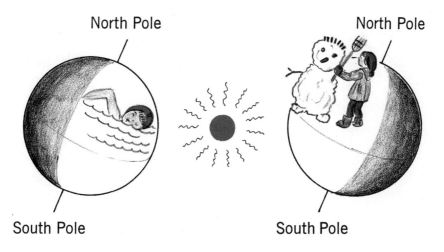

North Pole

North Pole

South Pole

South Pole

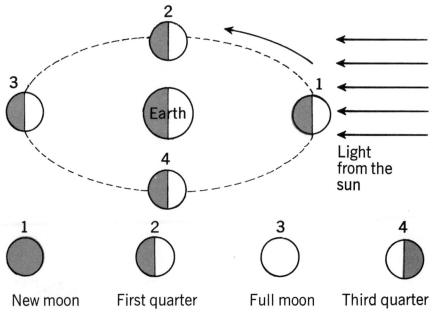

1	2	3	4
New moon	First quarter	Full moon	Third quarter

How the moon looks from the earth

The Month

If you look at the moon night after night, you can notice that its appearance keeps changing. One night it may look like a giant silver balloon. A few nights later it may look like a crescent roll. On another night you may see no moon at all, even though the sky is clear and the stars are out.

The moon does not make its own light. The light that makes the moon shine comes from the sun. Sunlight falls on the part of the moon that faces toward the sun. It is dark on the side of the moon that faces away from the sun.

The moon looks different from day to day because it

14

travels in a path around the earth, just as the earth travels in a path around the sun. As the moon travels around the earth, sometimes we see the side of the moon that faces toward the sun. This happens when the moon and the sun are on opposite sides of the earth. Then the moon looks like a shiny silver balloon. When the moon looks like this, we say there is a *full moon.* Sometimes we see the side of the moon that faces away from the sun. Then we see the dark side of the moon. This happens when the moon is between the earth and the sun. Then we can't see any light from the moon and we say there is a *new moon.* Sometimes we see only half of the side of the moon that faces toward the sun. Then we see only a *quarter moon.*

The new moon, the full moon and the quarter moons are called *phases* (FAY-zis) of the moon. The picture on page 14 shows how the phases follow each other as the moon moves around the earth. After the new moon we see more and more of the sunlit side of the moon until the full moon is seen. Then we see less and less of the sunlit side of the moon until it is a new moon again. Just before and just after a new moon, the moon is called a *crescent moon.*

The amount of time from one new moon to the next new moon is called a moon or *lunar* (LOON-er) month. A lunar month has about 29½ days.

The Parts Won't Fit

To make a calendar, we have to find an orderly plan to fit days into months and months into years. What would be the best kind of plan for a calendar?

In the best calendar, the year would be divided into a whole number of months. Then each new year would begin with a new month. In the best calendar, each year would be as long as a solar year so that each season would come during the same months each year. Then we would always know when to expect the seasons each year. In the best calendar, each month would be divided into a whole number of days. Then each month would always begin with a new day. In the best calendar, a calendar month would be as long as a lunar month. Then each month and each year would begin with the same phase of the moon.

It didn't take people long to find out that they couldn't make this kind of calendar. A calendar in which a calendar month is as long as a lunar month cannot have a whole number of days, because the lunar month has about 29½ days. A calendar in which the calendar year is as long as a solar year cannot have a whole number of lunar months. Twelve lunar months have about 354 days, but a solar year of about 365 days is about 12½ lunar months long.

Since people couldn't make the best kind of calendar,

they tried to make a calendar that was good at least in some ways. They could make each month about as long as a lunar month if they gave up the idea of having all months of the same length. They could make some months of the year 29 days long and as many months of the year 30 days long. If each 29-day month were followed by a 30-day month and each 30-day month were followed by a 29-day month, then each month would start with the same phase of the moon. A calendar built this way is called a *lunar calendar*.

They could make a calendar year about as long as a solar year if they gave up the idea of having each year begin with the same phase of the moon. A calendar built this way is called a *solar calendar*.

People had to decide what kind of calendar they wanted to use. In some places people made lunar calendars. In other places people made solar calendars. We shall find out what these calendars were like.

Rescuing cattle caught in a Nile River flood

The Egyptian Calendar

The Nile River flows through Egypt. Its valley is very fertile. For thousands of years Egyptians have done their farming in this fertile valley.

Farmers need water to make their crops grow. Even though rain hardly ever falls in the Nile valley, the valley farmers have had water for their crops. The water comes from the Nile when it floods its banks each year. The water is saved for irrigation.*

More than 5000 years ago the valley farmers found that they could tell when to expect the floods to come by the way the sky looked. They noticed that the floods came when the star Sirius and the sun rose at the same time. The noticed that this happened about every 365 days.

The Egyptians also noticed the regular changes in the phases of the moon. Because the moon was so easy to observe, the Egyptians at first used a lunar calendar. Ac-

* See *Irrigation* by the same authors, The John Day Company, New York.

cording to this calendar, each day began with sunrise. Each month began with the first full moon after sunrise. Each year began with the first new moon that followed the rising of Sirius with the sun at floodtime. Some years had 12 months, making a total of 354 days. But floodtime came about every 365 days. To make sure that floodtime came at about the same time in their calendar year, every few years the Egyptians put in a 13th month.

Later the Egyptians made a calendar with 12 months of 30 days each. This made the year only 360 days long. But they wanted to have a year with 365 days. So they put in 5 extra days at the end of the year to celebrate the birthdays of their five most important gods.

The five gods whose birthdays the Egyptians celebrated

FLOODTIME

SEEDTIME

HARVESTTIME

The Egyptians divided their year into three seasons of four months each. The seasons were floodtime, seedtime and harvesttime.

The Egyptians were among the first people to observe that the length of the solar year is 365¼ days. Even so, they still used their 365-day calendar. Under this calendar, floodtime kept coming later and later in the year. So, for a while, two New Year's Days were celebrated in Egypt. One New Year's Day was celebrated when the calendar year began. The other New Year's Day was celebrated on the first day of floodtime.

The Egyptians divided the period of time from sunrise

to sunset into 12 equal hours. They divided the period of time from sunset to sunrise into 12 equal hours, too. Because the number of hours of daylight was not always the same as the number of hours of darkness, a daylight hour did not always have the same length as a nighttime hour.

The Egyptians used a seven-day week. They probably learned to use the seven-day week from Jews who came to Egypt from western Asia, where the seven-day week was used. We shall see later how the Egyptians gave the days of the week the order we still use today.

On June 22, using the ancient Egyptian system, a daylight hour was one-third longer than a nighttime hour. It was 17 minutes longer, by our way of measuring time.

An Egyptian day divided into 12 daylight hours and 12 night-time hours

The Babylonian Calendar

Babylonia was an ancient country in the part of western Asia that is now know as Iraq. Two great rivers, the Tigris and the Euphrates, flowed through Babylonia, making its land very fertile. Like the Nile River, these rivers flooded their banks every year. Unlike the Nile floods, their floods did not occur at exactly the same time every year. Because the coming of the floods was not regular, the Babylonians could not use the start of flood-time as New Year's Day.

Like the Egyptians, the Babylonians noticed the regular changes in the phases of the moon. They began their month with the first appearance of a crescent moon. They began their year with the first crescent moon following the spring equinox. Their day began at sunset.

The Babylonians wanted to have a calendar that used lunar months. They knew that 12 lunar months added up to 354 days. At the same time they wanted to have a calendar year that was almost like a solar year. They did this by using a 19-year pattern for their calendar. Every period of 19 years had 12 years with 12 months and 7 years with 13 months. So 19 years had a total of 235 lunar months. But 235 lunar months had almost exactly the same number of days as 19 solar years. With this pattern, Babylonian New Year's Day always came at about the time of the spring equinox.

The Babylonians named their months after their gods. They used only twelve god-names. When a year had an extra month, one of the months was repeated.

The Babylonians may have been the first people to use the seven-day week and the day with 24 equal hours.

An ancient Babylonian religious festival. The star, the crescent and the sun were symbols of important Babylonian gods.

Stonehenge as it looks today

Other Ancient Calendars

Salisbury Plain is in the southern part of England. Standing on Salisbury Plain is a ring of great stones. Some of the stones are 30 feet high and weigh about 60 thousand pounds. This ring of stones is known as *Stonehenge.*

Stonehenge was built by people who lived in England about 4000 years ago. These people left no written record to help us learn about their customs and beliefs. Scientists have learned something about them, however, from Stonehenge. Stonehenge, they believe, helped serve as a calendar. Stonehenge helped serve as a calendar by the way the stones were placed. Lines connecting certain stones point to the most northerly place where the sun is ever seen to rise. The line drawn in the picture on page 25 shows where the sun rises around June 22. Then the sun is in its most northerly position. Lines connecting other stones point to the most southerly position of the sun. Lines connecting still other stones point to positions of the moon at special times. Using these lines, the Stone-hengers were able to keep track of the seasons and the years.

The ancient Chinese calendar was almost exactly like the calendar of ancient Babylonia. Their day, however, started at sunrise and their month started with the first sunrise before a new moon. The Chinese calendar following a 19-year pattern is even older than the ancient Babylonian calendar. In the Chinese calendar, 19 years was a period of time called a *chang*.

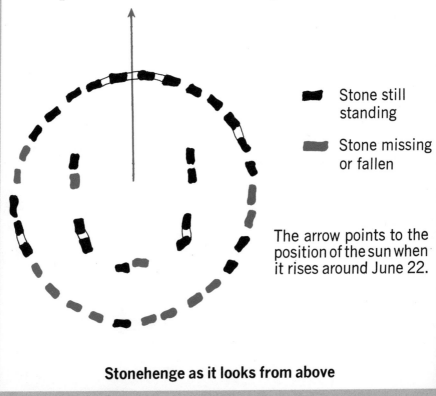

Stone still standing

Stone missing or fallen

The arrow points to the position of the sun when it rises around June 22.

Stonehenge as it looks from above

Romulus, the founder of Rome

Our Calendar's Great-grandfather

The calendar we use today is a great-grandchild of the calendar used in the ancient city of Rome about 2700 years ago. We know what this ancient calendar was like. But we do not know how much of the story of this calendar is fact and how much is myth.

According to myth, Rome was founded about 2700 years ago by Romulus, who was the son of Mars, the god of war. The mother of Romulus was descended from Venus, the goddess of love. Another name for Venus is Aphrodite. Romulus was the first king of Rome. He introduced the first Roman calendar.

The first Roman calendar had 10 months. Six months

26

had 30 days each and four months had 31 days each. This made a total of 304 days for the year. So the year in the first Roman calendar was about 61¼ days too short compared with the solar year.

March was the first month of this calendar. The other nine months, in order, were: April, May, June, Quintilis, Sextilis, September, October, November and December. April, June, Sextilis, September, November and December were all 30-day months. March, May, Quintilis and October were 31-day months. Some of the month names are like the month names we use today, but Quintilis and Sextilis look strange. Let us find out how the Romans named their ten months.

Name of month	Number of days in month
March	31
April	30
May	31
June	30
Quintilis	31
Sextilis	30
September	30
October	31
November	30
December	31

The ten months of the first Roman calendar

Naming the Months

The ancient Romans spoke a language called Latin. We have to know a little Latin and some of the Roman myths to understand how the months got their names. The chart below shows us how to count from one to ten in Latin:

Number	Number name	Pronunciation
1	unus	UN-us
2	duo	DOO-oh
3	tres	TRACE
4	quattuor	KWAT-war
5	quinque	KWIN-kwe
6	sex	SEX
7	septem	SEPT-em
8	octo	OCT-oh
9	novem	NO-wem
10	decem	DECK-em

Now look back at the list of month names on page 27. Quintilis is the fifth month. But the Latin word for five is *quinque.* So Quintilis got its name from the Latin word for five. In the same way, Sextilis, the sixth month, is named after *sex,* the Latin word for six, and so on.

The other four months got their names in a different way. Some scholars believe that March is named after Mars, the father of Romulus and the Roman god of war. They think that April is named after Aphrodite, the goddess of love, from whom Romulus was descended. They think that May is named after *majores* (my-OR-ays), the Latin word for elders or older ones. And they think that June is named after *juniores* (yune-YOUR-ays), the Latin word for younger ones.

Can you think of some English words that come from the Latin words we have listed?

The Year Gets Two More Months

The Romans soon found that their calendar year was much too short. Seasons and holidays came later and later in the year. A calendar like this was not a good guide to people for their religious or business affairs.

The second Roman king, Numa, changed the calendar

Numa, the second Roman king

January was named after Janus, the god of gates. He had two heads that looked in opposite directions at the same time.

by adding 51 days to the year. At the same time he added two new months to the year. He intended the new months to become the first and second months of the year. So he named the first month January, after the Roman god Janus (YON-uhs). Janus was the god of gates and doors. He had a head with two faces, so he could look in opposite directions at the same time. January was supposed to be the gate between the old year and the new year. The month after January was called February, after the Roman god Februus (FEB-roo-us). Februus was the god of purification. Even though Numa intended January and February to become the first and second months of the year, they were used as the eleventh and twelfth months instead. About 300 years after Numa's time, the year was begun with January, as Numa had intended, instead of March.

At the same time that Numa added two new months and 51 days to the year, he changed the number of days in some of the months. The Romans were very superstitious and they believed that even numbers were unlucky. The number 30 is an even number, so the Romans believed that the months with 30 days were unlucky months. Numa solved the problem of unlucky months by taking away one day from each of the six 30-day months. So April, June, Sextilis, September, November and December all became 29-day months. The number 29 is an odd number. March, May, Quintilis and October continued to have 31 days because the number 31 is an odd number, too. The six days that Numa took from the 30-day months and the 51 days he added to the year made a total of 57 extra days. He divided these 57 days between January and February. He gave January 29 days. This left 28 days for February. So February was the only month in the year with an even number of days.

Month	Number of days in month
March	31
April	29
May	31
June	29
Quintilis	31
September	29
October	31
November	29
December	29
January	29
February	28

Numa's twelve month calendar

The Romans Make More Changes

Numa's calendar of 355 days was too short. To keep Numa's year from falling behind the solar year, the Romans put in an extra month from time to time.

The extra month was usually added every other year. Sometimes the extra month had 27 days. Other times it had 28 days. Whenever the extra month was put in, it always followed February 23. Whenever the extra month was put in, the last five days of February were dropped. Now let us see how this scheme made Numa's calendar fit in with a solar year of 365½ days.

Suppose one year had 355 days. Then the next year would have an extra month of 27 days. But February lost 5 days when the extra month was added. So the second year would have only 27 − 5 or 22 extra days. This gave the second year a total of 355 + 22 or 377 days. The third year would have 355 days again. The fourth year would have 355 days and an extra month of 28 days, minus the 5 days that February lost. So the fourth year would have 23 extra days or a total of 355 + 23 or 378 days. The four years together had a total of 355 + 377 + 355 + 378 days or 1465 days. If the four years all had the same length, each year would have $\frac{1465}{4}$ days or 366¼ days. Each calendar year would be only one day longer than a solar year.

The priests decided when to put in the extra month. Sometimes they forgot to put it in. Sometimes they purposely left it out. After a few hundred years the extra month had been left out so often that January came in the fall instead of the winter!

Julius Caesar Comes to the Rescue

The calendar had to be corrected so that the seasons always came during the right months. Julius Caesar, who was emperor of Rome about 2000 years ago, took on the task of changing the calendar. He consulted an astronomer to find out what to do.

Julius Caesar

The first thing that had to be done was to bring the seasons back into the months where they belonged. This was done in the year 46 B.C. During this year an extra month of 28 days was added after February 23. As before, February lost its last 5 days when an extra month was added. So the extra month added only 23 days to the year. Then two more months with a total of 67 days were added. The three extra months that were put in that year added 23 + 67 days or 90 days to the year. So the year 46 B.C. had 445 days! It became known as the "year of confusion." Adding 90 days made the next year, 45 B.C., begin during the proper season.

The second thing that had to be done was to keep the seasons in the months where they belonged. This could be done if the calendar year had exactly the same number of days as the sun year. But a sun year has about 365¼ days and a calendar year had to have a whole number of days. The problem was solved by using a four-year pattern in which four calendar years have as many days as four solar years. The chart on page 35 shows how this was done.

This corrected calendar is known as the *Julian Calendar*, after Julius Caesar. It is a solar calendar. In this calendar, every fourth year has an extra day added to give it 366 days. A year with an extra day is called a *leap year*. In this calendar, January, March, May, Quintilis, Sextilis,

October and December are 31-day months. April, June, September and November are 30-day months. February has 28 days in an ordinary year. In a leap year, February has 29 days.

	Number of days in solar year	Number of days in calendar year
1st year	365¼	365
2nd year	365¼	365
3rd year	365¼	365
4th year	365¼	366
Total	1461	1461

In the year 44 B.C. the name of Quintilis was changed to July, to honor Julius Caesar. About fifty years later, the name of Sextilis was changed to August, to honor Augustus Caesar, the next emperor of Rome. Since the time of Augustus, there has been no change in the lengths or the names of the months.

A Roman farmer's calendar from the time of Augustus. It was carved on four slabs of stone, with three months on each slab. The picture for each month stands for the group of stars that rises and sets with the sun that month. The pictures are known as the signs of the zodiac. Another Roman calendar from this time is on page 1.

Ten Days That Were Lost

The Julian Calendar was good, but it wasn't good enough. It wasn't good enough because the sun year is actually 11 minutes and 14 seconds shorter than 365¼ days. A difference of 11 minutes and 14 seconds in a year doesn't seem like very much. However, after 400 years the difference added up to 3 days.

The trouble with the Julian Calendar was noticed when the church began to decide the date for Easter after the year A.D. 325. The date for Easter depends on the date of the first full moon after the spring equinox. As years passed, it was found that the spring equinox kept coming earlier and earlier in the year. This made it difficult to know exactly when Easter was supposed to come.

By the 16th century it was found that the spring equinox came 10 days earlier than it was supposed to on the calendar. So the church decided that the calendar had to be changed. Gregory XIII, who was the Pope at that time, suggested that a calendar prepared by an Italian doctor be used. The new calendar was designed to save 3 days every 400 years. It did this by changing the rules for setting leap years. Under the Julian Calendar, every fourth year was a leap year, when an extra day was added to February. Under the new calendar, this rule was followed *except* when the year could be divided by 100 but not by 400. So under the new calendar the years 1700, 1800, and 1900 were not leap years. The year 1600 was a leap year and the year 2000 will be a leap year, too. So 400 years by the new calendar were 3 days shorter than 400 years by the Julian Calendar. The new calendar is known as the *Gregorian Calendar*, after Pope Gregory.

Before the Gregorian Calendar could be used, the calendar and the seasons had to be brought into line. This was done by dropping 10 days from the calendar. The Pope ordered that the day that followed October 4, 1582, was to be called October 15, 1582.

Pope Gregory XIII

The Gregorian Calendar is used now in most of the countries of the world. It was not used in England and its colonies until 1752. When it was introduced in England, 11 days had to be dropped. There were angry demonstrations when this happened, and people rioted, shouting, "Give us back our eleven days!"

The Gregorian Calendar still isn't perfect. The calendar year is still too long. The mistake is so small, however, that it will add up to only 2 days, 14 hours and 24 minutes in 10,000 years.

An old picture of the creation according to the Bible. The days are numbered in Latin.

primo — first
secundo — second
tertio — third
quarto — fourth
quinto — fifth
sexto — sixth

The Seven-day Week

The day, the month and the year are periods of time that are based on natural events. However, people found they needed another unit of time that was longer than a day but shorter than a month. There was no natural period that they could use, so different units came into use in different countries. The early Babylonians divided the month into six periods of five days each. The early Egyptians divided the month into three *decans* of ten days each. The *fortnight*, a period of fourteen days is still used in England. The Julian Calendar and the Gregorian Calendar both use a *week* of seven days.

The seven-day week was first used in western Asia thousands of years ago. It was then adopted by the Jews who lived in western Asia. They, in turn, passed it on to the Egyptians and the Christians, from whom the Romans adopted it.

Why did the people of western Asia put seven days into a week? Some scholars think that the seven-day week is based on the four main phases of the moon. The month was divided into four seven-day periods. Each period began with a different phase of the moon. Other scholars think that we use a seven-day week because, according to the Bible, God made everything in the world in six days and rested on the seventh day.

Naming the Days of the Week

The ancient Greeks and Egyptians observed that the stars did not change their positions in the sky with respect to each other. However, they observed that seven bodies in the sky changed their positions or wandered among the stars. These bodies were the Sun, the Moon, Saturn, Mars, Jupiter, Venus and Mercury. They called these bodies *planets,* after the Greek word for wanderer. They named the wanderers after their gods. They believed that the planets moved in big circles around the earth.

The days of the week were named after the planets of the ancient Greeks and Egyptians. Sunday is named after the Sun. Monday is named after the Moon. Saturday is named after the god Saturn. Thursday is named after Thor. Thor was the name the ancient Germans had for the god Jupiter. Mars was known among the ancient Germans as Tiv, from which we get Tuesday. Venus was known as Frigg, from which Friday comes, and Mercury was known as Woden, from which Wednesday gets its name. The pictures on pages 41 and 42 are of some of these gods, as an artist imagined them.

The order of the days of the week comes from an Egyptian custom of about 1700 years ago. The Egyptians believed that each of the twenty-four hours of the day was protected by a planet. The order in which the planets were assigned as protectors depended on their distances from the earth. The chart on page 43 shows how the protectors were assigned to each hour of seven days in a row. The first hour of the first day was protected by the planet that the Egyptians believed was farthest away from the earth. This was Saturn. The second hour was protected by Jupiter or Thor, which they believed was the second most distant planet. The third hour was protected by Mars or Tiv, which was third in distance. The fourth hour was protected by the Sun, which was fourth in distance. The fifth hour was protected by Venus or Frigg, which was fifth in distance. The sixth hour was protected by Mercury or Woden, which was sixth in distance. And the seventh hour was protected by the Moon, which was closest to the earth. Each group of seven hours, after the seventh hour, had the same protectors as the first seven hours, in the same order. Using this scheme, the twenty-

Sun   **Moon**   **Tiv**

fourth hour had the same protector as the third hour. Its protector was Mars. This made the Sun the protector of the first hour of the second day.

The Egyptians also believed that each day had a special planet that ruled over it. The ruler for the day was the planet that protected the first hour of the day. Now look at the chart and find the rulers of each of the days of the week and the order in which they appear. To help you find them, they are printed in darker type. The rulers are, in order: Saturn, the Sun, the Moon, Tiv, Woden, Thor and Frigg. The days that belong to these planets are, in order: Saturday, Sunday, Monday, Tuesday, Wednesday, Thursday and Friday. This is the order of the days of the week of our calendar except that we now begin our week with Sunday and end it with Saturday.

Woden

Thor

Frigg

	The Protectors of the Hours of the Day						
	1st day	2nd day	3rd day	4th day	5th day	6th day	7th day
1st hour	**Saturn**	**Sun**	**Moon**	**Tiv**	**Woden**	**Thor**	**Frigg**
2nd hour	Thor	Frigg	Saturn	Sun	Moon	Tiv	Woden
3rd hour	Tiv	Woden	Thor	Frigg	Saturn	Sun	Moon
4th hour	Sun	Moon	Tiv	Woden	Thor	Frigg	Saturn
5th hour	Frigg	Saturn	Sun	Moon	Tiv	Woden	Thor
6th hour	Woden	Thor	Frigg	Saturn	Sun	Moon	Tiv
7th hour	Moon	Tiv	Woden	Thor	Frigg	Saturn	Sun
8th hour	Saturn	Sun	Moon	Tiv	Woden	Thor	Frigg
9th hour	Thor	Frigg	Saturn	Sun	Moon	Tiv	Woden
10th hour	Tiv	Woden	Thor	Frigg	Saturn	Sun	Moon
11th hour	Sun	Moon	Tiv	Woden	Thor	Frigg	Saturn
12th hour	Frigg	Saturn	Sun	Moon	Tiv	Woden	Thor
13th hour	Woden	Thor	Frigg	Saturn	Sun	Moon	Tiv
14th hour	Moon	Tiv	Woden	Thor	Frigg	Saturn	Sun
15th hour	Saturn	Sun	Moon	Tiv	Woden	Thor	Frigg
16th hour	Thor	Frigg	Saturn	Sun	Moon	Tiv	Woden
17th hour	Tiv	Woden	Thor	Frigg	Saturn	Sun	Moon
18th hour	Sun	Moon	Tiv	Woden	Thor	Frigg	Saturn
19th hour	Frigg	Saturn	Sun	Moon	Tiv	Woden	Thor
20th hour	Woden	Thor	Frigg	Saturn	Sun	Moon	Tiv
21st hour	Moon	Tiv	Woden	Thor	Frigg	Saturn	Sun
22nd hour	Saturn	Sun	Moon	Tiv	Woden	Thor	Frigg
23rd hour	Thor	Frigg	Saturn	Sun	Moon	Tiv	Woden
24th hour	Tiv	Woden	Thor	Frigg	Saturn	Sun	Moon

A Calendar That Is Good for Fifty Years

When you divide 365 days into weeks, you get 52 weeks with one day left over. So in the Gregorian Calendar, if a year begins on Monday, and it is not a leap year, the next year will begin on Tuesday. If it is a leap year, the next year will begin on Wednesday. That is why we need a new calendar each year.

Here the directions for making a calendar that is good for fifty years. Using a sheet of good quality white paper, trace the charts on pages 44 and 45. Then, on your traced copy, cut along the lines that are printed in red in the book. You will now have three separate parts of your 50-year calendar. The largest part will have three windows cut out of it. The rectangles printed in pink are where the windows will be. You will also have four slits. You cut the slits along the lines that are marked **AA, BB, CC** and **DD.**

						M						
		/				1	2	3	4	5	6	7
2	3	4	5	6	7	8	9	10	11	12	13	14
9	10	11	12	13	14	15	16	17	18	19	20	21
16	17	18	19	20	21	22	23	24	25	26	27	28
23	24	25	26	27	28	29	30	31				
30	31											

	OCT	JAN	
	MAY		
	AUG		
NOV	MAR	FEB	
	JUN		
	DEC	SEP	
	JUL	APR	Y
	OCT	JAN	
	MAY		
	AUG		
NOV	MAR	FEB	
	JUN		
	DEC	SEP	

A 50-YEAR CALENDAR

51	52B	52A	53	54	55	56B
56A	57	58	59	60B	60A	61
62	63	64B	64A	65	66	67
68B	68A	69	70	71	72B	72A
73	74	75	76B	76A	77	78
79	80B	80A	81	82	83	84B
84A	85	86	87	88B	88A	89
90	91	92B	92A	93	94	95
96B	96A	97	98	99		

A — B

CUT OUT

A — B

C — D

CUT OUT

SUN	MON	TUE	WED	THU	FRI	SAT

CUT OUT

C — D

In the leap years B means before March 1 and A means after Feb. 29.

Here is how to put your 50-year calendar together. Slip the narrowest strip (with the **Y** on it) through the slits marked **AA** and **BB,** so that you can see the names of the months through the top window. Slip the strip with the **M** on it through the slits marked **CC** and **DD,** so that you can see the days of the month through the bottom window. The picture on this page shows what your 50-year calendar looks like when it is put together.

Here is how to use your 50-year calendar. Suppose you want to know on what day of the week July 4 will fall in 1968. Slide the upper strip until the letter **Y** is under the year you want. In this case you will put the **Y** under the column where you see **68A**. This is because 1968 is a leap year. You use the column **68A** for all dates after February 29, 1968. For all dates in 1968 before March 1, you use the column where you see **68B**. Now slide the lower strip until the letter **M** is under the month

A 50-YEAR CALENDAR

In leap years,
B means before March 1
A means after February 29

you want. In this case you will put the **M** under July. The big window will show you what the calendar for July, 1968 looks like.

Your 50-year calendar always shows 31 days in a month. For a shorter month, ignore the extra days.

Some Other Calendars That People Use Today

The Gregorian Calendar is the official calendar of countries all over the world. But some religious groups use other calendars for religious purposes.

The Orthodox Eastern Church still uses the Julian Calendar. So when Greek Catholics celebrate Christmas, they celebrate it 13 days after Roman Catholics and Protestants do, because the Julian Calendar is now 13 days behind the Gregorian Calendar.

Jews use a calendar that is a lot like the calendar of the ancient Babylonians. Their day and month begin the way the Babylonian day and month did. To keep the Jewish spring holiday, Passover, in the proper season, the Jewish calendar follows a 19-year pattern like the Babylonian pattern. In a 13-month year, the 6th month, Adar, is repeated. The added month is called Veadar, or second Adar. The Jewish New Year comes in the fall.

Muslims, or Mohammedans, belong to the religion of Islam. They use a lunar calendar. The Islamic Calendar has 12 months with 29 or 30 days in each month. The Islamic Calendar follows a 30-year pattern. In every 30-year period there are 19 common years with 354 days in each year and 11 leap years with 355 days in each year. By the Islamic Calendar, a season comes later and later each year. After about 32 years, it is back in the same part of the year again.

About the Authors

IRVING and RUTH ADLER have written more than sixty books about science and mathematics. Dr. Adler has been an instructor in mathematics at Columbia University and at Bennington College, and was formerly head of the mathematics department of a New York City high school. Mrs. Adler, who formerly taught mathematics, science and art in schools in the New York area, recently also taught at Bennington. In addition to working with her husband writing this book, she has joined with him on 28 other titles in the *Reason Why* series and drawn the illustrations for most of them as well as for many other books written by him.

Books by Irving Adler alone and books by him in collaboration with Ruth Adler have been printed in 84 different foreign editions, in 14 languages and in 10 reprint editions.

The Adlers now live in the Town of Shaftsbury, near Bennington, Vermont.

QUESTIONS

Use your 50-year calendar to answer the following questions about the calendar month on pages 4 and 5. (Pay no attention to the dates of the phases of the moon.)

1. In what years does September 1st fall on Sunday? Why doesn't it fall on Sunday in 1980?
2. For what months in 1966 is this a correct calendar?
3. For how many months in 1970 is this the correct calendar? (Assume that extra days are disregarded.)

ANSWERS

1. 1952, 1957, 1963, 1968, 1974, 1985, 1991, 1996. Because 80A is not in the list of years above the Y when the calendar is set so that September 1 is on Sunday.
2. May.
3. Three. February, March and November.